RENEWAL
in
SONG

Compiled by Carol Perkins

James Boersma,
Editorial Consultant and Arranger

Wayne Hooper,
Engraver and Arranger

"Sing unto the Lord a new song."
Psalm 149:1

Perfect Binding $1.75
No. SB-72

Spiral Binding $2.50
No. SS-73

Sampler
Cassette $3.95

(Special Prices on Quanity Orders)

Logos International
Plainfield, New Jersey

Foreword

Since the turn of the century there has grown, with astounding vitality reminiscent of the early Church, a world-wide Spiritual Renewal in gigantic outpourings of the Holy Spirit. A fellowship of great joy has emerged, surpassing organizational boundaries. Resulting assemblages have expressed new spiritual fulfillment in music of a new religious dimension.

Many such groups have found enhanced reality in worship with frequent use of short, easily-remembered choruses. Thoughts are thus easily directed to God rather than to the printed page of the traditional verse-chorus hymn.

These songs should be selected in the service according to subject and their selection directed by the moving of the Holy Spirit; some are originally given by Him during the service. Often repetition of a chorus even several times greatly multiplies its worth.

Although a few other choruses loved by Renewal Christians have also been included in RENEWAL IN SONG, yet it is with choruses composed by them that this book is vitally concerned, and most of these are recent. Many of the composers preferred to remain anonymous because "These songs were born of the Spirit."

The following selected songs for adult or youth worship and praise are of varied subjects. They express descriptively this new "stirring in the land." Come, worship with us!

C.P.

All Over the World 1

Joyfully

All o-ver the world the Spir-it is mov-ing,

All o-ver the world, as the pro-phet said 'twould be.

All o-ver the world there's a might-y rev-e-la-tion

Of the glo-ry of the Lord, as the wa-ters cov-er the sea.

2. Deep down in my heart,

Thank You, Jesus 2

B. R.

Bob Robin

Thank you, Je-sus, thank you, Je-sus, For my heart has heard;

I am feed-ing, I am feed-ing On the liv-ing Word.

3   I Want to Drink at the Fountain

I want to drink, and drink at the foun - tain, at the
foun - tain, at the foun - tain. I want to drink, and
drink at the foun - tain, at the foun - tain of God's love.

2. Oh, won't you come and drink at the fountain.
3. I want to bring lost souls to the fountain.

4   Hallelujah!

Worshipfully

Hal - le - lu - jah, hal - le - lu - jah, hal - le - lu - jah, hal - le - lu - jah,

Fine

Hal - le - lu - jah, hal - le - lu - jah, hal - le - lu - jah, hal - le - lu - jah!

(D. C. al fine)

Hal - le - lu - jah, Hal - le - lu - jah, Hal - le - lu - jah, Hal - le - lu - jah!

His Praise Fills the Temple   5

J. W. H.

Jack W. Hayford

Worshipfully

His praise fills the tem - ple, His peace fills my heart, His joy

and His glo - ry He did won - drous - ly im - part. The

blest name of Je - sus brought me free - dom from sin.

Now His praise fills the tem - ple and His Spir - it dwells with - in.

He Is Lord   6

With consecration

He is Lord, He is Lord, He is ris - en from the dead and He is Lord;

Ev - ery knee shall bow, ev - ery tongue con - fess that Je - sus Christ is Lord.

7 Blessed Be the Lord God of Israel

Psalm 72:18,19

Shirley Powell

Bless-ed be the Lord God, the God of Is - ra - el, Bless-ed

be the Lord God, the God of Is - ra - el, Who on - ly do - eth

wond-rous things, Who on - ly do - eth wond-rous things and bless - ed

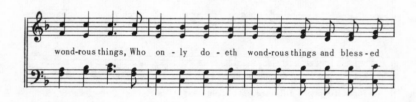

Fine

be His glo-rious name for - ev - er. And let the whole earth be

(D. C. al fine)

filled with His glo - ry, A - men, a - men, a - men, and a - men.

Used by permission

There's a River of Life

8

L.C.

L. Casebolt

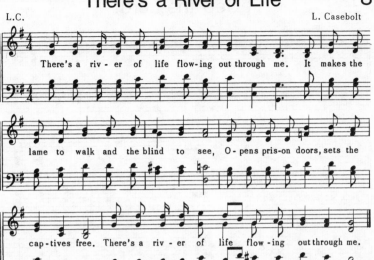

There's a riv-er of life flow-ing out through me. It makes the
lame to walk and the blind to see, O-pens pris-on doors, sets the
cap-tives free. There's a riv-er of life flow-ing out through me.

Arr. Copyright © 1971 by Joy Music Co. in "Renewal in Song."

We Worship and Adore Thee

9

We wor-ship and a-dore Thee, Fall-ing down be-fore Thee,
Songs of prais-es sing-ing, Hal-le-lu-jahs ring-ing. Hal - le-
lu-jah, Hal - le-lu-jah, Hal - le-lu-jah, A - men.

Arr. Copyright © 1971 by Joy Music Co. in "Renewal in Song."

10 I See the Lord!

Isaiah 6:1-3

I see the Lord, I see the Lord! He is high and lift - ed

up, and His train fills the tem - ple, He is high and lift - ed

up, and His train fills the tem - ple! And His an - gels cry, "Ho - ly!"

His an - gels cry, "Ho - ly!" His an - gels cry, "Ho - ly, is the Lord!"

11 Drain My Cup

B. R.   Bob Robin

Drain my cup of bit - ter - ness, Drain my cup of self - ish - ness;

Cleanse it, then, O Lord, cleanse me, And fill my cup all up with Thee.

Jesus Is His Name

With adoration

Je - sus is His name, yes, Je - sus is His name,

Je - sus is His name, my Je - sus. An - gels pros-trate fall and

crown Him Lord of all. Je - sus is His name, my Je - sus.

Arr. Copyright © 1971 by Joy Music Co. in "Renewal in Song."

Anointed

R. E. M.

R. Edward Miller

Worshipfully

An - oint - ed, an - oint - ed of the Fa - ther, Rose of Shar - on fair,

Lil - y of the val - ley; Love - ly, He's al - to - geth - er

love - ly, An - oint - ed, an - oint - ed of the Lord.

Used by permission

14 Miracles Can Happen

B. R.

Bob Robin

Mir - a - cles can hap - pen, and they're hap-pening now, Mir - a - cles can hap - pen, and they're hap - pening now. Je - sus Christ of Naz - 'reth still is just the same; Mir - a - cles are hap - pening in His name.

15 Break Up Your Fallow Ground

from Hosea 10:12

Break up your fal - low ground, let it rain, rain, rain. Break up your fal - low ground, let it rain, rain, rain. Break up your fal - low ground; Tear all your i - dols down. Je - sus is com - ing a - gain!

Make Mention That His Name Is Exalted

from Isa. 12:4-6

With Vigor

Make men-tion that His name is ex-alt-ed, Make

men-tion that His name is ex-alt-ed. He hath done

ex-cell-ent things, This is known in all the earth.

Cry out and shout, thou in-hab-i-tant of Zi-on,

Cry out and shout, thou in-hab-i-tant of Zi-on,

Great is the Ho-ly One, Great is the Ho-ly One of Is-ra-el!

17   O Lord, Let the Waters Roll

J.W.H.

Jack W. Hayford

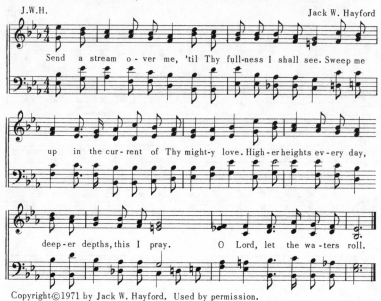

Send a stream o-ver me, 'til Thy full-ness I shall see. Sweep me
up in the cur-rent of Thy might-y love. High-er heights ev-ery day,
deep-er depths, this I pray. O Lord, let the wa-ters roll.

18   The Peace of God

D. D. L.

David D. Lindblad

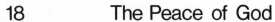

The peace of God that pass-es un-der-stand-ing, Be in your
heart a well of o-ver-flow-ing; Love to your fel-low man,
God's own cre-a-tion, The peace of God be with you ev-er-more.

His Riches In Glory 19

His rich - es in glo - ry so far be - yond meas - ure,
Then trust in the Sav - iour with all of thy heart,

Far be - yond meas - ure, far be - yond meas - ure; His
All of thy heart, all of thy heart; Then

rich - es in glo - ry so far be - yond meas - ure, Are
trust in the Sav - iour with all of thy heart, And

thine if thou wilt on - ly be - lieve.
faith shall be re - ward - ed to thee.

Arr. Copyright © 1971 by Joy Music Co. in "Renewal in Song."

Rejoice! 20

Joyfully

Re - joice, re - joice, re - joice, ye child - ren of the Lord! Re -

joice, re - joice, re - joice, re - joice, Re - joice, ye child - ren of the Lord!

2. Praise the Lord, 3. Clap your hands,

Arr. Copyright © 1971 by Joy Music Co. in "Renewal in Song."

21   Heavenly Father, I Appreciate You

Worshipfully

Heav - en - ly Fa - ther, I ap - pre - ci - ate you,
Son of God, I mag - ni - fy you,
Ho - ly Spir - it, You're a com - fort to me,

Heav - en - ly Fa - ther, I ap - pre - ci - ate you.
Son of God, I mag - ni - fy you.
Ho - ly Spir - it, You're a com - fort to me.

I love you, a - dore you, I bow down be - fore you.
My Sav - iour, you saved me, a new life you gave me.
You lead me, you guide me, you stay close be - side me.

Heav - en - ly Fa - ther, I ap - pre - ci - ate you.
Son of God, I mag - ni - fy you.
Ho - ly Spir - it, you're a com - fort to me.

Arr. Copyright © 1971 by Joy Music Co. in "Renewal in Song."

22   Holy Is the Lord

Reverently

Ho - ly is the Lord and might - y is His name; King of heaven, yet

(continued)

down to earth He came. An - gels sing His praise, all earth shall

do the same; Ho - ly is the Lord and might - y is His name!

Call Unto Me 23

Jeremiah 33:3

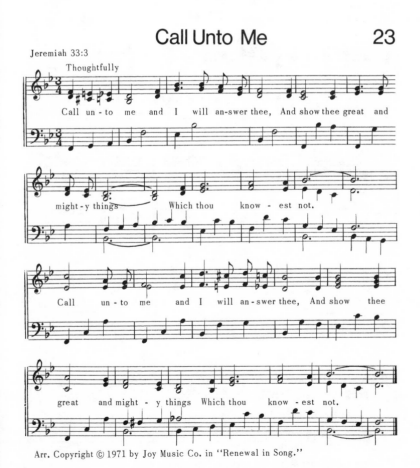

Thoughtfully

Call un - to me and I will an-swer thee, And show thee great and

might - y things Which thou know - est not.

Call un - to me and I will an-swer thee, And show thee

great and might - y things Which thou know - est not.

24 It Is the Time to Take the Kingdom!

L.C.

L. Casebolt

It is the time to take the king-dom! Rise up, ye strong, 'Tis Christ's com-mand. For ev-ery pow'r and do-min-ion Is giv-en now in-to your hand. He that hath ears to hear the trum-pet, He that hath heart to un-der-stand, It is the time to take the king-dom! Rise up, ye strong, pos-sess the land!

Singing "Glory! Hallelujah!" 25

P. S. C.

Phyllis C. Spiers

Sing-ing "Glo-ry! Hal-le-lu-jah!" Sing-ing glo-ry a-round the throne;

Wav-ing palms with loud hos-an-nas, For the mar-riage of the Lamb is come.

This Is the Hour of Miracles 26

J. W. H.

Jack W. Hayford

With confidence

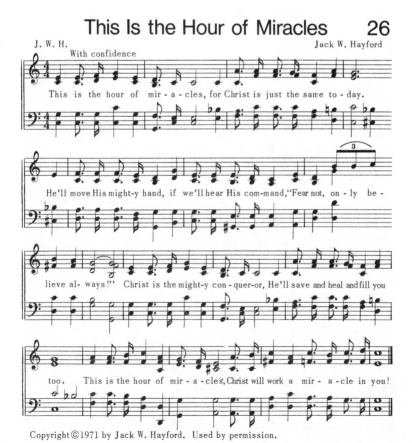

This is the hour of mir-a-cles, for Christ is just the same to-day.

He'll move His might-y hand, if we'll hear His com-mand, "Fear not, on-ly be-

lieve al-ways!" Christ is the might-y con-quer-or, He'll save and heal and fill you

too. This is the hour of mir-a-cles, Christ will work a mir-a-cle in you!

27 His Name Is As Ointment Poured Forth

from Sol. 1:3

A. C.

A. Cadman

Worshipfully

His Name is as oint-ment poured forth, Je - sus,

Je - sus, Je - sus, Je - sus. His Name is as

oint-ment poured forth, His Name is as oint-ment poured forth.

Arr. Copyright © 1971 by Joy Music Co. in "Renewal in Song."

28 What a Mighty God We Serve!

With Strength

What a might-y God we serve, What a might-y

God we serve! An - gels bow be - fore Him,

Heaven and earth a - dore Him. What a might-y God we serve!

Arr. Copyright © 1971 by Joy Music Co. in "Renewal in Song."

In a New and Living Way

Reverently

In a new and liv-ing way, Je-sus, come to us to-day;

Bless the bread, and bless the wine, Bless each one, make us

whol-ly Thine. Si-lent-ly, sweet Spir-it, come, Cause each yearn-ing

heart to say, My Lord has come in a new and liv-ing way.

God Is Moving Again

God is mov-ing a-gain, God is mov-ing a-gain;

His king-dom is com-ing in pow-er, God is mov-ing a-gain!

31 Walk in the Light

I John 1:7

David D. Lindblad

If we walk in the light as He is in the light,

We have fel - low-ship one with an - oth - er

And the blood of Je - sus Christ cleans - es ev - er - y sin,

If we walk in the light as He is in the light.

32 Abba, Father

B. R. from Rom. 8:15,16

Bob Robin

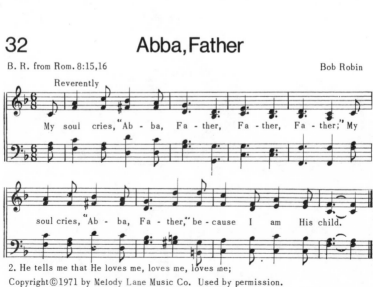

Reverently

My soul cries, "Ab - ba, Fa - ther, Fa - ther, Fa - ther;" My

soul cries, "Ab - ba, Fa - ther," be - cause I am His child.

2. He tells me that He loves me, loves me, loves me;

From Glory to Glory He's Changing Me

from II Cor. 3:18

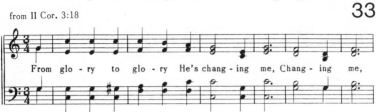

From glo - ry to glo - ry He's chang - ing me, Chang - ing me,

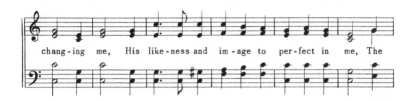

chang - ing me, His like - ness and im - age to per - fect in me, The

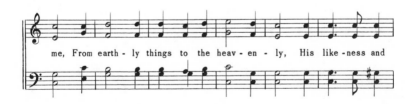

love of God shown to the world. For He's chang - ing, chang - ing

me, From earth - ly things to the heav - en - ly, His like - ness and

im - age to per - fect in me, The love of God shown to the world.

Arr. Copyright © 1971 by Joy Music Co. in "Renewal in Song."

34 Lord, Make Us One

P. C. S.

Phyllis C. Spiers

Lord, make us one, Lord, make us one, Lord, make us one ev - ery-where;

Lord, make us one, Lord, make us one, Lord, make us one ev - ery-where.

35 Therefore With Joy Shall Ye Draw Water

Isaiah 12:3,4

Joyfully

There-fore with joy shall ye draw wat - er out of the wells of sal -

va - tion, And in that day shall ye say, "Praise the Lord!"

There - fore with joy shall ye draw wat - er out of the wells of sal -

va - tion, And in that day shall ye say, "Praise the Lord!"

The Day of Thy Power

36

J. W. H.

Worshipfully

Jack W. Hayford

May I stand, O Lord, in this ho - ly place; May I wor - ship
Thee, and be - hold Thy face; May I be trans-formed by Thy
Word and Thy Spir - it, and be - hold the day of Thy power!

The Breath of God

37

W. E. B. - C.

Worshipfully

Wm. E. Booth - Clibborn

Let it breathe on me, let it breathe on me, Let this
breath of God now breathe on me; Let it breathe on me,
let it breathe on me, Let this breath of God now breathe on me.

38 Thou Art Worthy!

Rev. 4:11

Pauline Michael Mills

Worshipfully

Thou art wor-thy, Thou art wor-thy, Thou art wor-thy, O Lord; Thou art wor-thy to re-ceive glo-ry, Glo-ry and hon-or and pow'r! For Thou hast cre-a-ted, hast all things cre-a-ted, For Thou hast cre-a-ted all things, And for Thy pleas-ure they are cre-a-ted: Thou art wor-thy, O Lord!

Open Wide Ye Gates 39

from Psalm 24:7,10

Mary Lou Neal

O-pen wide ye gates and be ye lift-ed up ye doors, And the King of glo-ry shall come in! Who is this King of glo-ry? He is the Lord of hosts. O-pen wide ye gates and be ye lift-ed up ye doors!

I Must Have Jesus in My Whole Life 40

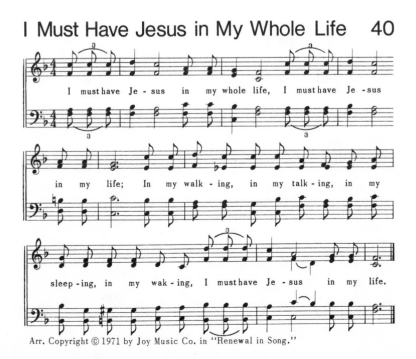

I must have Je-sus in my whole life, I must have Je-sus in my life; In my walk-ing, in my talk-ing, in my sleep-ing, in my wak-ing, I must have Je-sus in my life.

41 O Cloud of Great Glory

R. E. M.

R. Edward Miller

Worshipfully

O cloud of great glo-ry, the Pres-ence of God, De-scend now in

Spir-it on wings as a dove. O cloud of great glo-ry, the

Pres-ence of God, De-scend now and hov-er o-ver me.

Used by permission

42 Into the Hands
That Were Wounded to Save Me

With consecration

In-to the hands that were wound-ed to save me, In-to the

hands that are might-y to help, In-to the hands that will

guide me and guard me, Sav-iour, my life I give.

Worthy Is the Lord! 43

Wor-thy is the Lord, and wor-thy to be praised! Wor-thy is the Lord, and wor-thy to be praised! Wor-thy, Oh, wor-thy is the Lord!

For God So Loved the World 44

D. D. L. from John 3:16

David D. Linblad

For God so loved the world, That He gave His on-ly Son.

For God so loved the world, That He came from hea-ven a-bove.

For God so loved the world, That e-ter-nal life He gave.

For God so loved the world, Oh sin-ner, won't you be saved!

45   I Love You, Jesus

With adoration

I love you, Je - sus, I love you, Je - sus, I love you,

Je - sus, and I al - ways will. and I al - ways will.

Arr. Copyright © 1971 by Joy Music Co. in "Renewal in Song."

46
God Is Great and Greatly to Be Praised

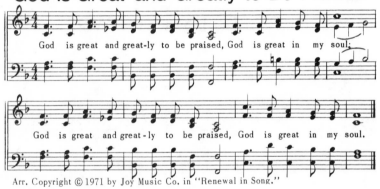

God is great and great-ly to be praised, God is great in my soul;

God is great and great-ly to be praised, God is great in my soul.

Arr. Copyright © 1971 by Joy Music Co. in "Renewal in Song."

47   Oh, Deeper Yet

Oh, deep-er yet I pray, dear Lord, Oh, take me deep - er still, Till

I am lost in Thee, dear Lord, And I know Thy bless-ed per - fect will.

Arr. Copyright © 1971 by Joy Music Co. in "Renewal in Song."

I Will Bless the Lord At All Times 48

Psalm 34:1-4

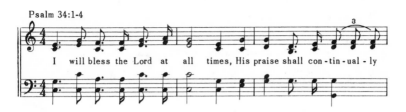

I will bless the Lord at all times, His praise shall con-tin-ual-ly

be in my mouth; My soul shall make her boast in the Lord, The

hum-ble shall hear there-of and be glad. Oh, mag-ni-fy the Lord with

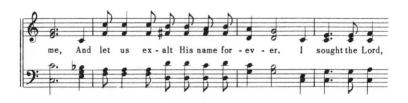

me, And let us ex-alt His name for-ev-er. I sought the Lord,

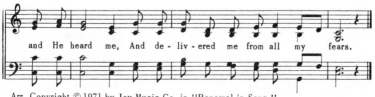

and He heard me, And de-liv-ered me from all my fears.

49 I Am the Way, the Truth and the Life

from John 14:6

"I am the way, the truth and the life," That's what Je-sus said;

"I am the way, the truth and the life," That's what Je - sus said.

With - out the way, there is no go - ing, With - out the truth, there

is no know - ing, With - out the life, there is no grow - ing.

(D.S. * al fine)

50 Let There Be Singing

M. L. N.

Mary Lou Neal

Let there be sing - ing, let there be joy,

Let there be praise in the house of the Lord;

(continued)

Let there be mer-cy, re-joice, re-joice! We're build-ed to-geth-er a house for the Lord.

Life, So Rich and Abundant   51

Life, so rich and a-bun-dant, Joy, so full and tri-um-phant,

Peace, that no-thing can mar And no man take a-way;

Light, no shad-ow of turn-ing, Oil, still keep-ing me burn-ing,

Oh, this won-der of won-ders, Je-sus is mine!

52   He Is My Jesus

M. S.

Marialice Smith

He is my Je - sus, O love - ly One; He is my

Je - sus, O pre - cious One. He died on Cal - v'ry

to set me free. He is my Je - sus, e - ter - nal - ly.

53   A Boundless, Eternal Supply

B. R.

Bob Robin

With Joy

He gave you a drink and you'll nev - er thirst, He gave you His

life and you'll nev - er die; On man - na you're fed, on the

liv - ing bread - A bound - less, e - ter - nal sup - ply.

His Yoke Is Easy

R. E. H.

R. E. Hudson

His yoke is eas - y, His bur - den light; I've found it so, I've found it so;

He lead - eth me by day and by night, Where liv - ing wa - ters flow.

54

Wonderful Jesus!

B. A. B.

Benjamin A. Baur

With adoration.

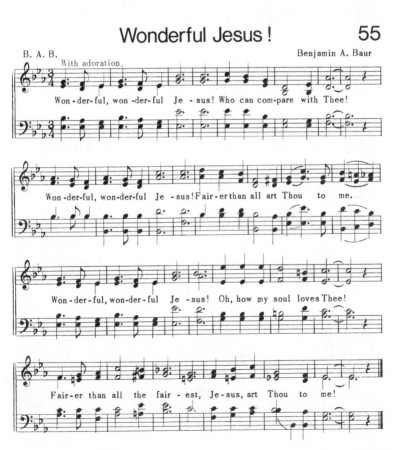

Won - der - ful, won - der - ful Je - sus! Who can com - pare with Thee!

Won - der - ful, won - der - ful Je - sus! Fair - er than all art Thou to me.

Won - der - ful, won - der - ful Je - sus! Oh, how my soul loves Thee!

Fair - er than all the fair - est, Je - sus, art Thou to me!

55

56   This Is My Rest Forever

From Psalm 132:13-16

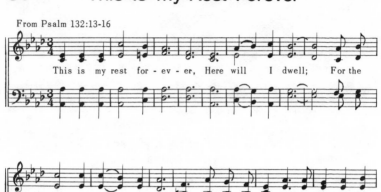

This is my rest for - ev - er, Here will I dwell; For the

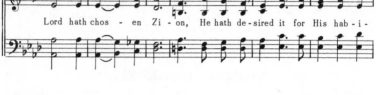

Lord hath chos - en Zi - on, He hath de - sired it for His hab - i -

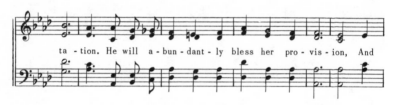

ta - tion. He will a - bun - dant - ly bless her pro - vis - ion, And

sat - is - fy her poor with bread; He will clothe her

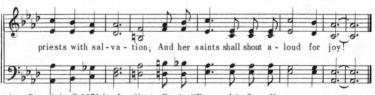

priests with sal - va - tion; And her saints shall shout a - loud for joy!

Fresh Oil from the Throne 57

E. S.

Eleanor Stern

Fresh oil from the throne, fresh oil from the throne, A - noint us to -
day with fresh oil from the throne. We need the pow - er
in this last hour. A - noint us to - day with fresh oil from the throne.

Praise Waiteth For Thee 58

from Psalm 65:1

Lionel Maddaford

Praise wait - eth for Thee, O Lord, Praise wait - eth for Thee;
Praise wait - eth for Thee, O Lord, Wait - eth for Thee in Zi - on.

59 Thou Mighty Christ

A. A. A.

A. A. Anderson

With consecration

Thou might-y Christ, come forth in me. My will and way I yield to Thee. The bar-ren sings a tra-vail-ing song. Oh praise His name, it won't be long!

60 My Redeemer and Saviour Divine

O. B.

Oscar Backlund

With His pre-cious blood He has cleansed me. He has filled me and made me whole. He's en-dued me with Ho-ly Ghost pow-er, Touched my spir-it and bod-y and soul.

Jesus Is All To Me

61

D. M.

Doug Moody

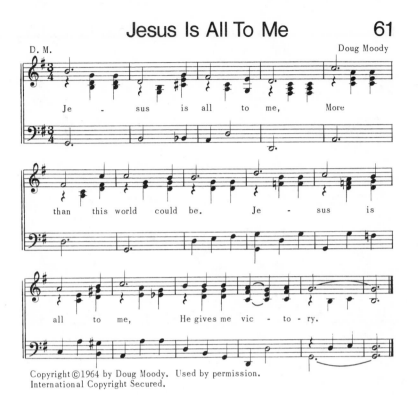

Je - sus is all to me, More
than this world could be. Je - sus is
all to me, He gives me vic - to - ry.

Oh Come, Let Us Adore Him

62

With praise

Wade's Cantus Diversi

1. Oh come, let us a - dore Him, Oh come, let us a - dore Him,
2. We'll give Him all the glo - ry, We'll give Him all the glo - ry,
3. We'll praise His name for - ev - er, We'll praise His name for - ev - er,

Oh come, let us a - dore Him,
We'll give Him all the glo - ry,
We'll praise His name for - ev - er,

Christ, the Lord.

63 I Was Glad When They Said Unto Me

Psalm 122:1

I was glad when they said un-to me, I was
glad when they said un-to me, I was glad when they said
un-to me, "Let us go in-to the house of the Lord."

Arr. Copyright © 1971 by Joy Music Co. in "Renewal in Song."

64 One Touch

L. G.

Lorraine Gaglardi

One touch   is all that I need, One touch   will set my soul free;
One touch   One touch

One touch   is all that I need, One touch,   one touch.(one touch)
One touch   One touch,

Used by permission

We'll Work Till Jesus Comes 65

Elizabeth Mills

William Miller

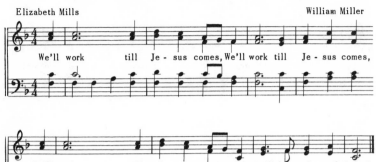

We'll work till Je-sus comes, We'll work till Je-sus comes,

We'll work till Je-sus comes and we'll be gath-ered home!

2. We'll pray 3. We'll sing

Oh, God Is Good 66

African Origin

Oh, God is good, Yes, God is good, Oh, God is good; He is good to me.

2. God cares for me, 3. God leads me on, 4. I'll do His will,

Arr. Copyright © 1971 by Joy Music Co. in "Renewal in Song."

I'll Say "Yes, Yes, Yes" 67

I'll say "Yes, yes, yes;" I'll say "Yes, yes, yes;" I'll say

"Yes, Lord," I'll say "Yes, Lord, I'll say "Yes, yes, yes."

Arr. Copyright © 1971 by Joy Music Co. in "Renewal in Song."

68 Abiding in the Vine

from John 15:4

I found a new way of liv - ing, I found a new life di - vine,

I have the fruit of the Spir - it; I'm a - bid-ing, a - bid-ing in the

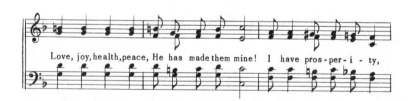

vine. A - bid-ing in the vine, A - bid-ing in the vine;

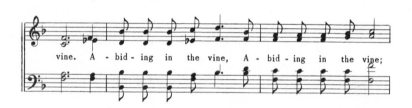

Love, joy, health, peace, He has made them mine! I have pros-per-i - ty,

pow - er and vic - to - ry, A - bid-ing a - bid-ing in the vine.

There Shall Be Deliverance in Zion 69

J. B. from Obadiah 1:17

Jane Brown

There shall be de - liv-erance in Zi - on, There shall be de - liv-erance in Zi - on, There shall be de - liv-erance in Zi - on, And my peo - ple shall be set free! Set free, set free! And my peo - ple shall be set free!

Used by permission

I've Got Peace Like a River 70

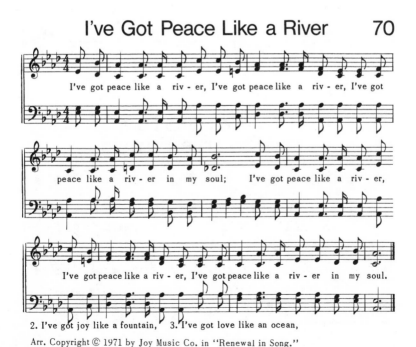

I've got peace like a riv - er, I've got peace like a riv - er, I've got peace like a riv - er in my soul; I've got peace like a riv - er, I've got peace like a riv - er, I've got peace like a riv - er in my soul.

2. I've got joy like a fountain, 3. I've got love like an ocean,

71 It's Only By Thy Spirit

B. R.

Bob Robin

It's on - ly by Thy Spir - it, Lord, that I am led to Thee,

It's on - ly by Thy Spir - it, Lord, my eyes are made to see;

It's not by might and not by power, but in re - al - i - ty,

It's on - ly by Thy Spir - it, Lord, that I am led to Thee.

72 I Will Bless the Lord From This Time Forward

I will bless the Lord from this time for - ward, Ev - en now and for - ev - er -

more. I will bless the Lord from this time for - ward, Ev - en now and for -

(continued)

ev - er - more. Praise the Lord, praise the Lord, praise the Lord, praise the Lord! I will

bless the Lord from this time for - ward, Ev - en now and for - ev - er - more.

Sing, O Sing Unto the Lord 73

from Isa. 12:4,5

Sing, Oh sing un - to the Lord, Sing and praise His ho - ly name;

Sing, Oh sing un - to the Lord, Sing and praise His ho - ly name!

Make men - tion that His name is ex - al - ted, Let it be known thru all the

earth! Sing, Oh sing un - to the Lord, Sing and praise His ho - ly name!

74   His Banner Over Me Is Love

From Song of Sol. 2:4; 6:3

He brought me to the ban-quet-ing ta - ble And His ban-ner o - ver

me is love, He brought me to the ban-quet-ing ta - ble And His ban-ner

o - ver me is love, He brought me to the ban-quet-ing ta - ble And His

ban-ner o - ver me is love, His ban-ner o - ver me is love.

2. I am my beloved's and He is mine, etc.

Arr. Copyright © 1971 by Joy Music Co. in "Renewal in Song."

75   Oh, the Blood of Jesus

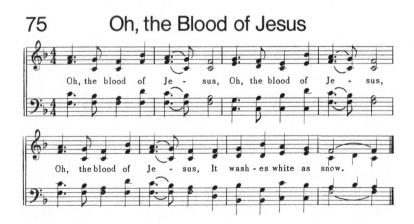

Oh, the blood of Je - sus, Oh, the blood of Je - sus,

Oh, the blood of Je - sus, It wash - es white as snow.

Renew a Right Spirit In Me   76

B. R. from Psalm 51:10

Bob Robin

with dedication

Re - new a right spir - it in me to - day, Re - new a right pur - pose in me, I pray. Re - new my first love, make it warm and true As the first love I knew.

Copyright ©1971 by Melody Lane Music Co. Used by permission.

Isn't He Wonderful!   77

Is - n't He won - der - ful, won - der - ful, won - der - ful, Is - n't Je - sus, my Lord, won - der - ful! Eyes have seen, ears have heard, It's re - cord - ed in His Word, Is - n't Je - sus, my Lord, won - der - ful!

Arr. Copyright ©1971 by Joy Music Co. in "Renewal in Song."

78 If God Be For Us

A. S M. from Rom. 8:31

Aimee Semple McPherson

If God be for us, who can be a - gainst? If God be for us, who can be a - gainst? If God be for us, who can be a - gainst? He that is with us might - ier is than all that be a - gainst!

79 Yet I Will Rejoice

Hab. 3:18   With joy

Yet I will re - joice, re - joice in the Lord, Yet I will re - joice, re - joice in the Lord, Yet I will re - joice, re - joice in the Lord, And joy in - the God of my sal - va - tion.

Make Me More Like Thee 80

With dedication

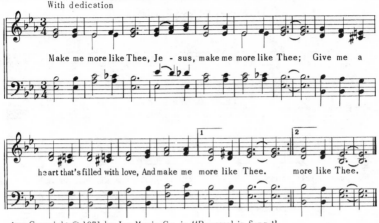

Make me more like Thee, Je - sus, make me more like Thee; Give me a

heart that's filled with love, And make me more like Thee. more like Thee.

Ask, Seek and Knock 81

from Matt. 7:7

If you ask, keep on ask - ing; If you seek, keep on seek - ing;

If you knock, keep on knock - ing and be - lieve. For if you

ask and keep on ask - ing, If you seek and keep on

seek - ing, If you knock and keep on knock - ing, you'll re - ceive.

82
All Things Are Possible
When We Believe

from Mark 9:23

83 If You Know Jesus, Then Testify

H. J. & R. J.

Harry and Richard Jump

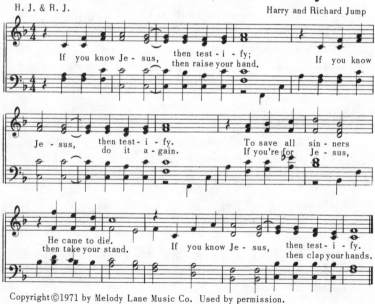

Jesus Is Here 84

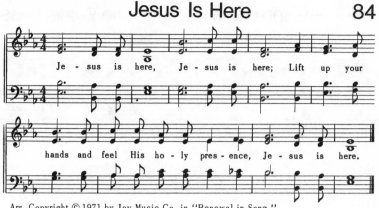

Je - sus is here, Je - sus is here; Lift up your

hands and feel His ho - ly pres - ence, Je - sus is here.

Let's Go Up To Zion 85

With joy

Let's go up to Zi - on, Let's go up to Zi - on,

Let's go up to Zi - on, the cit - y of our God.

2. There's singing up in Zion, 3. There's clapping, 4. There's praising,

86
I Love Him Best of All

A. S.   Arthur Slater

I love Him, I love Him, I love Him best of all;

I love Him, I love Him, I love Him best of all.

87
He Can Spread a Table in the Wilderness

from Psalm 78:19

Confidently

He can spread a table in the wild-der-ness, He can spread a
table for you. He can spread a table in the wil-der-ness,
And that's what He's go-ing to do. So lift up your voice and
praise Him, and praise Him, and praise Him. There's no oth-er God be-
side Him, Who can spread a table for you. He can spread a
table in the wil-der-ness, And that's what He's go-ing to do!

If You Abide In Me

88

J. C. from John 15:7

Jerry Cook

If you a-bide in me and my words a-bide in you, Ye shall

ask what ye will, it shall be done un-to you. For the en-e-my must flee;

There is joy and vic-to-ry, When you a-bide in me.

Lovely Name, Jesus

89

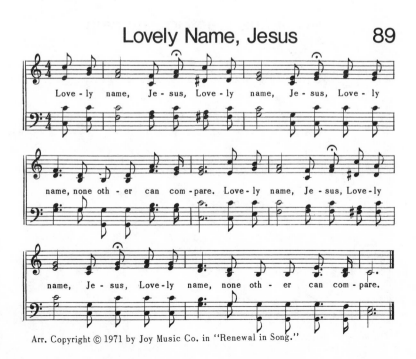

Love-ly name, Je-sus, Love-ly name, Je-sus, Love-ly

name, none oth-er can com-pare. Love-ly name, Je-sus, Love-ly

name, Je-sus, Love-ly name, none oth-er can com-pare.

90 Love One Another

Love one an-oth-er and you will see A new light shin-ing in thee; Love one an-oth-er and you will see A new light shin-ing in thee.

May repeat this measure twice

91 My Jesus Can Do Anything

B. L. G.   Bonnie L. Green

My Je-sus can do an-y-thing, There's noth-ing too hard for Him. He has con-quered sin, His vic-t'ry I'll tell; I know in Him that all is well. My Je-sus can do an-y-thing, There's no-thing too hard for Him.

What the World Needs Is Jesus 92

B. A. B.

Benjamin A. Baur

What the world needs is Je - sus, Just a glimpse of Him;

What the world needs is Je - sus, Just a glimpse of Him;

He will bring joy and glad - ness, Take 'a - way sin and sad - ness;

What the world needs is Je - sus, Just a glimpse of Him.

I Love Him 93

Stephen Foster

I love Him, I love Him, Be - cause He first loved me,

And pur - chased my sal - va - tion on Cal - v'ry's tree.

94 There's Never Been a Day Like This Day

Joyfully

There's nev-er been a day like this day to me. There's nev-er been a day like this day I see There nev-er was a light that shin-eth so bright as this day, this glo-ri-ous day!

95 Coming This Way

Com-ing this way, yes, com-ing this way, A might-y re-viv-al is com-ing this way. Keep on be-liev-ing, trust and o-bey, For a might-y re-viv-al is com-ing this way.

Joy in the Morning

B. R.

Bob Robin

Joy in the morning and joy at night, Joy in the noon-day and in twi-light,

Joy with-out ceas-ing, un-speak-a - bly, Joy God has giv-en to me!

Copyright © 1971 by Melody Lane Music Co. Used by permission.

2. Peace like a river so wide and deep,
   All through my waking, or when asleep,
   Peace and contentment eternally,
   Peace God has given to me.

3. Love for our Lord, and love for each one,
   Love is the key - through God the Son,
   Love is the answer so mar-v'lously,
   Love God has given to me.

Hallelujah! Jesus is Coming Again 97

P. C. S.

Phyllis C. Spiers

Hal-le - lu - jah! hal-le - lu - jah! Je-sus is com-ing, He's com -ing a - gain;

Hal - le - lu - jah! Hal-le - lu - jah! Je-sus is com-ing a -gain.

2. Are you ready, are you ready, etc.   3. Yes, I'm ready, yes, I'm ready, etc.

Copyright © 1949 by Phyllis C. Spiers in "Spiritual Songs by the Spiers."
Used by permission.

98 The Law of the Lord is Perfect

Psalm 19:7-11

Verse 7: The law of the Lord is perfect, con-vert-ing the soul:-
Verse 8: The statutes of the Lord are right, re-joic-ing the heart:
Verse 9: The fear of the Lord is clean, en-dur-ing for - ev - er:

The tes- ti - mo -ny of the Lord is sure, mak-ing wise the sim-ple.
The com-mand-ment of the Lord is pure, en-light-en-ing the eyes,
The judg-ments of the Lord are true, and righteous al-to-geth- er.

Refrain

Verse 10: More to be de-sired are they than gold, yea, than much fine gold:

(D. C.)

Sweet- er al - so than hon - ey, and the hon - ey- comb.

Coda

Verse 11: More - ov - er by them is thy ser-vant warned, is thy ser-vant warned:

And in keep-ing of them — — is great re - ward.

There's a Mighty Glory Coming  99

There's a might - y glo - ry com - ing, And it's com - ing in our day and it's com-ing now to stay. There's a might - y glo - ry com - ing, And it's com-ing from the pres-ence of the Lord.

Arr. Copyright © 1971 by Joy Music Co. in "Renewal in Song."

When Your Cup Runneth Over With Joy 100

W. B.-C.

William Booth-Clibborn

Joyfully

When your cup run - neth o - ver with joy, When your cup run - neth o - ver with joy, You find it eas - y to pray And to sing all the day When your cup run - neth o - ver with joy.

Copyright © 1949, renewal, by Wm. Booth-Clibborn, owner. Used by permission.

101 Just So Many Hours

B. R. Raise the key ½ step for each verse
Bob Robin

There's just so man - y hours in a day, There's just so
man - y hours in a day, So man - y hours to pray and to
walk the nar - row way. There's just so man - y hours in a day.

2. There's just so many days in a year,
   There's just so many days in a year,
   So many days that we can be as He'd have us be.
   There's just so many days in a year.

3. There's just so many years in a life,
   There's just so many years in a life,
   So many years to live, and your life for Jesus give.
   There's just so many years in a life.

4. Oh, heaven it will last eternally,
   Oh, heaven it will last eternally,
   When eons here are done, heaven's time has just begun.
   Oh, heaven it will last eternally.

102 Send a Mighty Stream

J. W. H.
Jack W. Hayford

Send a might - y stream surg - ing in my soul. By Thy Ho - ly

(continued)

Spir - it, Lord, take full con - trol. Mas - ter ev - ery fear,

con - quer ev - ery doubt, Send a sweet re - fresh - ing, Purge with - in, with - out.

Show Us Thy Glory, O Lord 103

Show us Thy glo - ry, O Lord; Show us Thy

glo - ry, O Lord. May the dew of Heav - en bring

us re - fresh - ing, And show us Thy glo - ry, O Lord.

104   It's All in Thee

It's all in Thee, Lord, it's all in Thee, Bless-ing and pow-er and lib-er-ty. Oh, let Thy Spir-it sweep o-ver me. It's all in Thee, Lord, it's all in Thee.

105   Filled With God

With consecration

Filled with God, yes, filled with God, Par-doned and cleansed and filled with God; Filled with God, yes filled with God, Emp-tied of self, and filled with God.

I'm So Glad I Belong to Jesus   106

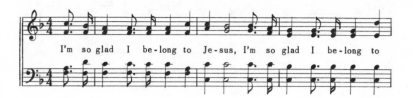

I'm so glad I be-long to Je-sus, I'm so glad I be-long to

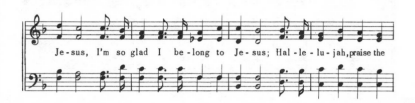

Je-sus, I'm so glad I be-long to Je-sus; Hal-le-lu-jah, praise the

Lord! Praise the Lord,   praise the Lord,   Praise the
a - men, a - men,   a - men, a - men,

Lord,   praise the Lord;   Praise the Lord,
a - men, a - men,   a - men, a - men;   a - men, a - men,

praise the Lord,   Hal - le - lu - jah, praise the Lord!
a - men, a - men,

107 Jesus Breaks Every Fetter

Slowly

1. Je - sus breaks ev - ery fet - ter, Je - sus breaks ev - ery
2. I will shout Hal - le - lu - jah! I will shout Hal - le -
3. I will give God the glo - ry, I will give God the

fet - ter, Je - sus breaks ev - ery fet - ter, And He sets me free.
lu - jah! I will shout Hal - le - lu - jah! For He sets me free.
glo - ry, I will give God the glo - ry, For He sets me free.

108 How Great Is Our God!

How great is our God, How great is His name;

He's the great - est One, For - ev - er the same!

He rolled back the wat - ers of the might - y Red Sea,

And He says, I will lead you, "Put your trust in me."

Arr. Copyright © 1971 by Joy Music Co. in "Renewal in Song."

I Want More of Jesus 109

I want more of Je-sus, More and more and more; I want more of
Je-sus than I ev-er had be-fore. I want more of His great love so
rich and full and free; I want more of Je-sus, and He wants more of me.

Arr. Copyright © 1971 by Joy Music Co. in "Renewal in Song."

There's a Way Through 110

There's a way through, there's a way through; Vic-t'ry is
cer-tain, God's prom-ise is true. There's a way through, there's a way
through; Je-sus, my Sav-iour, will nev-er fail you.

Arr. Copyright © 1971 by Joy Music Co. in "Renewal in Song."

111 The Lord Hath Done Great Things

from Psalm 126:1-3

Jack W. Hayford

When the Lord turned a-gain our cap-tiv-i-ty, Then were we as those that dream; And the ones who heard, with won-der said, The Lord hath done great things. So our mouths are filled with laugh-ter, And our tongues with sing-ing praise, For the Lord hath done great things for us where-of we are glad, For the Lord hath done great things for us where-of we are glad.

Shut In With God 112

W. G.

William Grum

Shut in with God in a se -cret place, There in the Spir-it be-hold-ing His face, Gain-ing new pow-er to run in the race, I long to be shut in with God.

Cause Me to Come to Thy River 113

R. E. M.

R. Edward Miller

Cause me to come to Thy riv - er, O Lord. Cause me to drink of Thy riv - er, O Lord. Cause me to live by Thy riv - er, O Lord. Cause me to come, Cause me to drink, Cause me to live.

114 Confidence

J. W. H. from Phil. 1:6

Jack W. Hayford

Brightly

Say, have you heard the en-cour-ag-ing word that brings con-fi-dence?

God will con-tin-ue what He start-ed in you, have con-fi-dence.

Un-til the mo-ment Christ ap-pear-eth and the clouds all roll a-way,

You can be sure that His pow'r will se-cure you, have con-fi-dence to-day.

115 I Feel Like Traveling On

Yes, I feel like trav-el-ing on, I feel like trav-el-ing on, trav-el-ing on,

on. My heav'nly home is bright and fair, I feel like trav-el-ing on.
trav-el-ing on.

Oh, It Is Jesus

Worshipfully

Oh, it is Je-sus, Yes, it is Je-sus, Oh, it is Je-sus in my soul,
Oh, I will praise Him, Yes, I will praise Him, Oh, I will praise Him in my soul,

For I have touched the hem of His gar-ment, And His blood has made me whole.

Oh, For a Mighty Outpouring

P. C. S.

Phyllis C. Spiers

Oh, for a might-y out-pour-ing! Send it on ev-ery heart;

Oh, for the Ho-ly Ghost stir-ring, In my hun-gry heart let it

start. Purge a-way all that would hin-der, Cause me to seek Thee a-fresh;

O-pen the flood-gates of heav-en, Come, and Thy peo-ple now bless.

118 A Stream Is Flowing

A. A. A.

A. A. Anderson

A stream is flow - ing from Cal - va - ry,

A stream is flow - ing, it cleans - seth me;

From sin and shame, in Je - sus' name,

A stream is flow - ing from Cal - va - ry.

119 This Father of Mine

B. R.

Bob Robin

This Fa - ther of mine, this Fa - ther of mine,

Holds all of this world in His hands di - vine;

(continued)

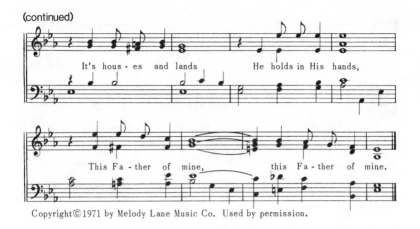

It's hous - es and lands He holds in His hands,

This Fa - ther of mine, this Fa - ther of mine.

I Want to Be Real 120

A. A. A.   With Consecration   A. A. Anderson

I want to be real, Lord, I want to be real;

Re - move ev - ery doubt, Lord, I want to be real.

Thou see - st my heart, Thou know'st ev - ery part.

I want to be real, Lord, I want to be real.

121
With Stammering Lips and Another Tongue

From Isa. 28:11

Bob Robin

2. As calves in a stall shall they all feed together,
3. The Word of the Lord shall be precious amongst them,

Rejoice in the Lord

B. C.

Barbara Cook

122

With joy

Re - joice in the Lord, re - joice ev - er - more; Great is our

God! De - light in His Word and pray in His name;

Ye shall have joy! In Thy pres - ence is

ful - ness of joy; At Thy right hand pleasures ev - er - more.

At Thy right hand pleas - ures ev - er - more.
(D. C. al Fine)

123 His Name Shall Be Called Wonderful!

from Isa. 9:6

Jan Sibelius

With Praise

His name, His name shall be called Won - der - ful; His name, His name shall be called Coun - sel - or; The might - y God, the Ev - er - last - ing Fa - ther, the Prince of Peace, through - out e - ter - ni - ty; The might - y God, the ev - er - last - ing Fa - ther, the Prince of Peace, through - out e - ter - ni - ty!

Arr. Copyright © 1971 by Joy Music Co. in "Renewal in Song."

124 My Lord Is Real

My Lord is real, yes, real to me; My Lord is real, yes, real to me.

(continued)

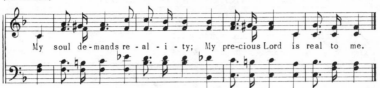

My soul de-mands re - al - i - ty; My pre-cious Lord is real to me.

Trust in the Lord With All Thy Heart 125

Prov. 3:5-8

Roy Hicks, Jr.

Trust in the Lord with all thy heart; Lean not un - to thy -

self. In all thy ways ac - know - ledge Him;

He shall di - rect thy paths. Be not wise in

thine own eyes, Fear the Lord and 'de - part from e - vil;

This shall be health and strength to thee. Trust in the Lord to - day!

Give Me Oil in My Lamp

Give me oil in my lamp, keep me burn- ing, Give me

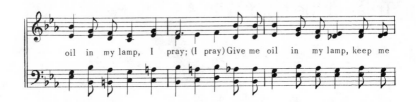

oil in my lamp, I pray; (I pray) Give me oil in my lamp, keep me

burn- ing, (keep me burn-ing) Keep me burn-ing till the break of day.

Sing ho-san-na, Sing ho-san-na, Sing ho-san-na to the King of Kings;
Sing, Sing, Sing, Sing;

Sing ho-san-na, Sing ho-san-na, Sing ho-san-na to the King!
Sing, Sing, Sing, Sing!

This Is the Year of Jubilee   127

from Lev. 27:24

With strength

This is the year of Ju-bi-lee, This is the year of Ju-bi-lee, When all the cap-tives are set free. Come, ye halt, ye blind, ye lame, Leap and shout for joy a-gain! This is the year of Ju-bi-lee!

Arr. Copyright © 1971 by Joy Music Co. in "Renewal in Song."

Let the Oppressed Go Free!   128

J. B. from Isa. 58:6

James Beall

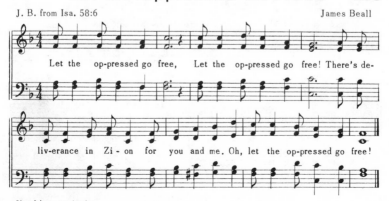

Let the op-pressed go free, Let the op-pressed go free! There's de-liv-erance in Zi-on for you and me. Oh, let the op-pressed go free!

Used by permission

129 Oh, Glory, Glory, Glory!

With joy

1. Oh, glo - ry, glo - ry, glo - ry, Oh, glo - ry to the Lamb! Oh, Hal - le - lu - jah!
2. On Sun - day I am hap - py, On Mon - day full of joy, On Tues - day I have

I am saved and I'm so glad I am. Oh, glo - ry, glo - ry, glo - ry, Oh,
peace with - in that noth - ing can des - troy; On Wednesday and on Thursday I'm

glo - ry to the Lamb! Hal - le - lu - jah! I am saved and bound for the hap - py land.
walk - ing in the light, Oh, Fri - day is a heav'n be - low and Sat - ur - day's al - ways bright.

Arr. Copyright © 1971 by Joy Music Co. in "Renewal in Song."

130 I Will Praise Him

M. J. H.

Mrs. M. J. Harris

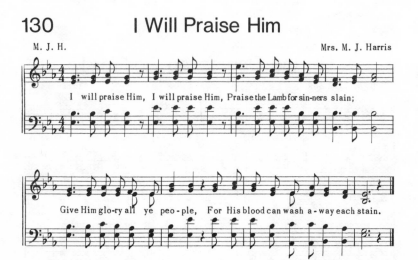

I will praise Him, I will praise Him, Praise the Lamb for sin - ners slain;

Give Him glo - ry all ye peo - ple, For His blood can wash a - way each stain.

Wonderful Name! 131

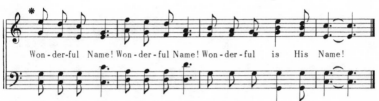

Won - der - ful Name! Won - der - ful Name! Heal-ing and life are in His Name!

Won - der - ful Name! Won - der - ful Name! Won - der - ful is His Name!

The two choruses on this page may be sung consecutively, or simultaneously, and each can be sung as a round if divided at this sign ✲

Wonderful! 132

I. S.   Iris Sutherland

Won - der - ful! Won - der - ful! Won - der - ful is His Name!

Won - der - ful! Won - der - ful! Won - der - ful is His Name!

133   Exceedingly Abundantly

from Eph. 3:20

Ex - ceed-ing a - bund-ant - ly a - bove all we ask or think,

That's what my God can do! Ex - ceed-ing a - bund-ant - ly a-

bove all we ask or think, That's what He'll do for you! He can save and

He can heal; I'm so glad I know He's real. Ex - ceed-ing a-

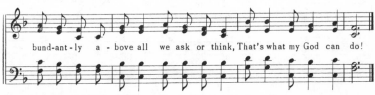

bund-ant - ly a - bove all we ask or think, That's what my God can do!

When He Comes 134

I'm going to run, run, run to meet my Je - sus, I'm going to

run, run, run to meet my Je - sus, I'm going to run, run,

run to meet my Je - sus, When He comes, when He comes.

2. Every eye shall then behold Him,   4. Every knee shall bow before Him,
3. Every tongue shall then confess Him, 5. I'm going to sing, sing, sing, Oh Hallelujah,

Arr. Copyright © 1971 by Joy Music Co. in "Renewal in Song."

Trust in the Lord and Don't Despair 135

Trust in the Lord and don't de-spair, He is a Friend so true;

No mat - ter what your trou - bles are, Je - sus will see you through.

Arr. Copyright © 1971 by Joy Music Co. in "Renewal in Song."

136   Bless Thy Word

B. R.

Bob Robin

Bless thy word, O Ho - ly Spir - it, O - pen Thou our hearts to Thee;

Speak thy truth, Oh, may we hear it, O - pen Thou our eyes to see.

137   It's No Longer I That Liveth

Gal. 2:20

It's no long - er I that liv - eth, But Christ that

liv - eth in me! It's no long - er I that liv - eth, But

Christ that liv - eth in me! He lives, He lives, Christ is a - live in me!

It's no long - er I that liv - eth, But Christ that liv - eth in me!

So Little Time

T. P.

Tim Peterson

So lit - tle time to win the lost to Him; So lit - tle
time - the days are grow - ing dim. Our Lord is com - ing, O glo-ri-ous
day! But men are dy - ing, Time is slip - ing a - way.

Used by permission

Call on the Name of the Lord

R. H. Jr.

Roy Hicks, Jr.

Call on the name of the Lord, Call on the
name of the Lord, That your sins be for - giv - en and your
bo - dy be made whole; Call on the name of the Lord.

Used by permission

140 He Hears and He'll Answer

B. R.

Bob Robin

He hears and He'll an - swer each whis - pered prayer. He hears and He'll an - swer, for He doth care. If you'll on - ly trust Him, He'll car - ry you through. He hears and He'll an - swer you.

Copyright ©1971 by Melody Lane Music Co. Used by permission.

141 Wonderful and Marvelous

Wond-er -ful and mar -vel-ous is Je - sus to me; Sweet-er than the hon-ey from the hon - ey-comb is He. Je-sus is real, He'll nev-er fail. I will praise Him now and thru-out all e - ter - ni - ty.

Arr. Copyright © 1971 by Joy Music Co. in "Renewal in Song."

Greater Is He That Is Within You 142

1 John 4:4

Great - er is He that is with - in you Than he that is

in the world, Great - er is He that is with - in you

Than he that is in the world; Great - er than

an - gels or pow - ers, Great - er than this life or death,

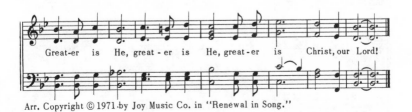

Great-er is He, great - er is He, great - er is Christ, our Lord!

Arr. Copyright © 1971 by Joy Music Co. in "Renewal in Song."

143   Get Down at Jesus' Feet

If you want to know the pow'r of God, Get down at Je - sus' feet;

If you want to know the pow'r of God, Get down at Je - sus' feet.

Get down, broth-er, get down, sis - ter, get down at Je - sus' feet;

Get down, sin - ner, get down, saint, get down at Je - sus' feet.

144   We Live Because of You

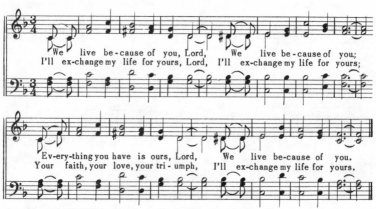

We live be-cause of you, Lord,   We live be-cause of you;
I'll ex-change my life for yours, Lord, I'll ex-change my life for yours;

Ev-ery-thing you have is ours, Lord,   We live be-cause of you.
Your faith, your love, your tri - umph, I'll ex-change my life for yours.

He's In My Heart 145

B. L. G.

Bonnie L. Green

He's in my heart, He's in my heart; He's rul - ing there in ev - ery part. He cleansed my sin and en-tered in. Now Je-sus is in my heart.

Every Knee Shall Bow 146

B. R.

Bob Robin

Ev - ery knee shall bow, ev - ery tongue shall con - fess, On - ly Je - sus has true right-eous-ness. He is all I need, no-thing more or less. On - ly Je - sus has true right - eous-ness.

147 I'm Glad I'm Yours

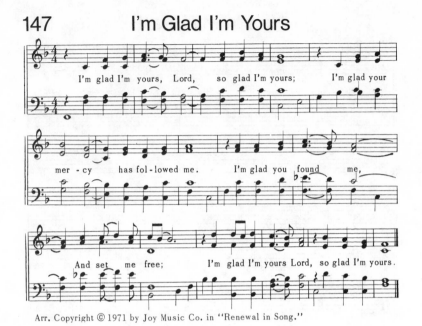

I'm glad I'm yours, Lord, so glad I'm yours; I'm glad your mer-cy has fol-lowed me. I'm glad you found me, And set me free; I'm glad I'm yours Lord, so glad I'm yours.

148 I'll Praise His Name For Evermore

C. P. D.   Cyril P. Dawes

I'll praise His name for ev-er-more, I'll praise His name for ev-er-more; I'll praise, I'll praise, I'll praise, I'll praise, I'll praise His name for ev-er-more.

I Have Decided to Follow Jesus 149

I have de - cid - ed to fol - low Je - sus, I have de -
cid - ed to fol - low Je - sus, I have de - cid - ed to fol - low
Je - sus; I won't turn back, I won't turn back.

Arr. Copyright © 1971 by Joy Music Co. in "Renewal in Song."

2. Take the whole world, but give me Jesus; I won't turn back,

3. The cross before me, the world behind me; I won't turn back,

4. I am feasting on milk and honey; It satisfies,

Nothing Between 150

C. A. Tindley
Arr. by F. A. Clark

C. A. T. With consecration

Noth - ing between my soul and the Sav - iour, So that His blessed face may be seen;

Nothing preventing the least of His fav - or, Keep the way clear, let noth - ing be - tween.

151   I Am Coming

I am com-ing while the hand of God is on me, I am coming while the Spir-it moves my soul, I am com-ing while the pre-cious blood is flow-ing; I sur-rend-er and let Je-sus take con-trol.

152   There's Been a Great Change in Me

There's been a great change in me, a great change in me, I am so hap-py and I am so free! He brought me out of bond-age in-to His lib-er-ty. Oh, a great change in me!

Take Your Burdens to Calvary 153

D. D. L.

David D. Lindblad

Take your bur - dens to Cal - va - ry, What - ev - er

they may be; Take your bur - dens to Cal - va - ry,

Friend, you will see. He'll an - swer ev - ery re -

quest of yours, And give you faith a - new!

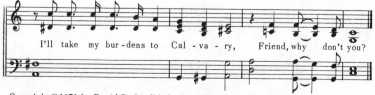

I'll take my bur - dens to Cal - va - ry, Friend, why don't you?

Oh, to Be Like Thee!

T. O. Chisholm

Wm. J. Kirkpatrick

Oh, to be like Thee! Oh, to be like Thee, Bless-ed Re-
deem-er, pure as Thou art! Come in Thy sweet-ness, come in Thy
full-ness; Stamp Thine own im-age deep on my heart.

155 Yesterday, Today, Forever

A. B. Simpson

J. H. Burke

Yes-ter-day, to-day, for-ev-er, Je-sus is the same; All may change but
Je-sus nev-er Glo-ry to His name! Glo-ry to His name! Glo-ry
to His name! All may change, but Je-sus nev-er. Glo-ry to His name!

You Can't Outgive the Lord   156

B. R.
Bob Robin

You can't out-give the Lord, no mat-ter what you do. You'll

find that in the end, the Lord's out-giv-en you. In

ev-ery-thing you give of love and ser-vice true, You

can't out-give the Lord, no mat-ter what you do.

Oh, Magnify the Name of the Lord!   157

Oh, mag-ni - fy the name of the Lord! Oh mag-ni - fy the name of the Lord!

Sing ye a - loud and a - dore Him Oh, mag-ni - fy the name of the Lord!

158 It's a Lovely, Lovely Name

Joyfully

It's a love-ly, love-ly name, the name of Je - sus,

It's a love-ly, love-ly name from heav-en a - bove;

Dis - pell-ing the clouds of doubt and fear, Fill -ing my sad-dened

heart with cheer, It's a love-ly, love-ly name, the name I love.

Arr. Copyright © 1971 by Joy Music Co. in "Renewal in Song."

159 You're Not Your Own, You're His

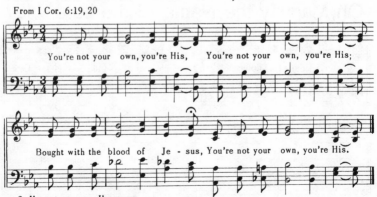

From I Cor. 6:19, 20

You're not your own, you're His, You're not your own, you're His;

Bought with the blood of Je - sus, You're not your own, you're His.

2. I'm not my own, I'm yours,
Arr. Copyright © 1971 by Joy Music Co. in "Renewal in Song."

160
Whosoever Will to the Lord May Come

Who - so - ev - er will to the Lord may come, Who - so - ev - er

will to the Lord may come, Who - so - ev - er will to the

Lord may come, He'll not turn one a - way. Je - sus, (Je - sus)

Je - sus (Je - sus) heals the brok - en heart - ed; Je - sus, (Je - sus)

Je - sus (Je - sus) heals the brok - en heart - ed; Je - sus, (Je - sus)

Je - sus (Je - sus) heals the brok - en heart - ed. He will set you free!

Arr. Copyright © 1971 by Joy Music Co. in "Renewal in Song."

161 Rivers Shall Flow in the Wilderness

Riv - ers shall flow in the wild - er - ness, Floods from hea - ven de - scend; And the earth shall be filled with His Ho - ly - ness, For - ev - er, world with - out end.

162
Jesus Brought the Sunshine Back Again

Joyfully

Je - sus brought the sun - shine back a - gain, Taught my trem - bling heart to sing a - gain, Took a - way my fears and gave me joy di - vine. Now ev - ery - thing that Je - sus bought for me is mine!

More Than Anyone Else 163

More than an-y-one else, I want to see Je-sus;

I want to see Him Who suf-fered for me.

Safe in His arms, I'll praise and a-dore Him,

And tell Him I love Him More than an-y-one else.

Hallelujah! 'Tis Done! 164

P. P. B.

P. P. Bliss

With confidence

Hal-le-lu-jah, 'tis done! I be-lieve on the son;

I am saved by the blood of the Cru-ci-fied One. fied One.

165 I Love Him, I Love Him, I Love Him

With devotion

I love Him, I love Him, I love Him; He's the
Rose of Shar - on to me. I love Him, I
love Him, I love Him; And some day His face I shall see.

166 Sweep Over My Soul

Sweep o - ver my soul, sweep o - ver my soul, Sweet Spir - it, sweep
o - ver my soul. My rest is com - plete, when I
sit at His feet. Sweet Spir - it, sweep o - ver my soul.

We'll Give the Glory to Jesus   167

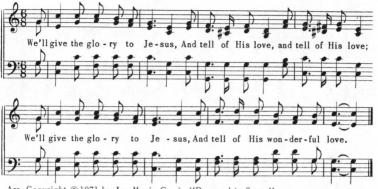

We'll give the glo-ry to Je-sus, And tell of His love, and tell of His love;

We'll give the glo-ry to Je-sus, And tell of His won-der-ful love.

The Lord of Harvest   168

J. F. from Luke 10:2

Jackie Forrester

The Lord of Har-vest is call-ing un-to you;

The task is great, the la-bor-ers are few.

Oh Lord, I'm wea-ry and there's so much yet to do.

He whis-pers, "Come and I will strength-en you."

169   This Is My Commandment

from John 15:12, I John 1:4

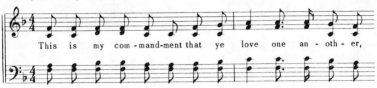

This is my com-mand-ment that ye love one an - oth - er,

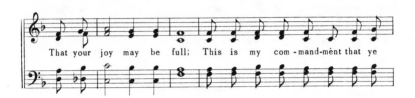

That your joy may be full; This is my com-mand-ment that ye

love one an - oth - er, That your joy may be full. That your joy may be

full,   That your joy may be full, This is my com-

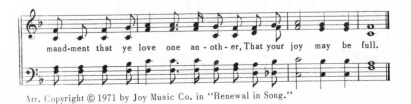

mand-ment that ye love one an - oth - er, That your joy may be full.

He Is Worthy to Be Praised 170

He is wor-thy to be praised, He is wor-thy to be praised! He's the Lord of glo-ry, the An-cient of days. He is wor-thy to be praised!

Arr. Copyright © 1971 by Joy Music Co. in "Renewal in Song."

Victory! Victory! 171

W. B.-C.

William Booth-Clibborn

With strength

Vic-to-ry! Vic-to-ry! O-ver all the powers of
Vic-to-ry! Vic-to-ry!
dark-ness, vic-to-ry! When the bat-tle's in ar-ray, An-gels
help us in the fray, And God fights for those who pray, Vic-to-ry!

Used by permission

172 Spring Up, O Well

from Numbers 21:17

Spring up, O well, with-in my soul; Spring up, O
well, and o-ver-flow. Spring up, O well,
flow out from me; Spring up, O well, and set me free!
set oth-ers free!

173 Roll Off Your Burdens

B. R.

Bob Robin

With Confidence

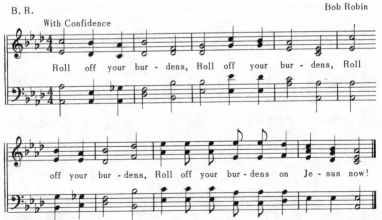

Roll off your bur-dens, Roll off your bur-dens, Roll
off your bur-dens, Roll off your bur-dens on Je-sus now!

2. He wants to save you, 3. He wants to heal you, 4. He wants to fill you,

Magnify the Lord With Me   174

A. T.

A. Tee

Mag - ni - fy the Lord with me, Bless-ed Lamb of Cal - va - ry,

For His grace so rich and free Mag - ni - fy the Lord with me.

Mag - ni - fy the Lord with me, Bless-ed Lamb of Cal - va - ry,

Je - sus gives us lib - er - ty. Oh, mag - ni - fy the Lord with me.

Oh, How I Love Jesus   175

Isaac Watts from I John 4:19

Stephen Jones

Oh, how I love Je - sus, Oh, how I love Je - sus,

Oh, how I love Je - sus, be - cause He first loved me.

176 Let Me Glory in the Lord

Let me glo - ry in the Lord, Let me glo - ry in the Lord. Let my one de - sire be to lift my Je - sus high - er, Let me glo - ry in the Lord.

177 Just To Have a Touch, Lord, From You

Just to have a touch, Lord, from you, To help with the trials I go through. Tho' dark may be the night, It brings a ray of light, When I have a touch, Lord, from you.

Ready 178

S. E. L.

Charlie D. Tillman

With consecration

Read-y to go, read-y to stay, Read-y my place to fill;

Read-y for ser-vice, low-ly or great, Read-y to do His will.

I Know God's Promise Is True 179

C. H. M.

Mrs C. H. Morris

Tis true, Oh yes, tis true, God's won-der-ful
the pro-mise is true,

pro-mise is true, For I've trust-ed and test-ed, and
tis true,

tried it, And I know God's pro-mise is true.
tis true.

180 The Old Time Religion

Give me that old-time re-li-gion, Give me that old-time re-li-gion, Give me that old-time re-li-gion, And it's good e-nough for me.

2. It was good for my father,   3. It was good for Paul and Silas,
4. It will take us all to heaven,

181 In the Name of Jesus

Maori origin

Forcefully

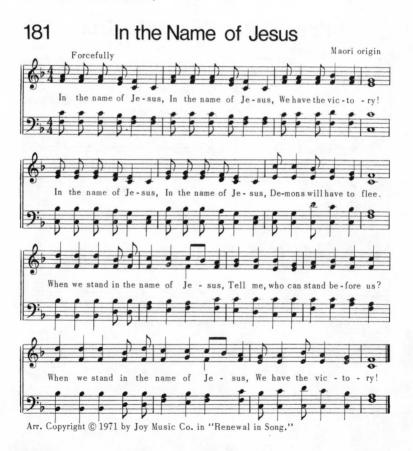

In the name of Je-sus, In the name of Je-sus, We have the vic-to-ry!

In the name of Je-sus, In the name of Je-sus, De-mons will have to flee.

When we stand in the name of Je-sus, Tell me, who can stand be-fore us?

When we stand in the name of Je-sus, We have the vic-to-ry!

Don't Lose the Joy
of the Lord in Your Soul

182

P. P.

Penny Piester

With joy

Don't lose the joy of the Lord in your soul, For the joy of the

Lord is your strength. Yield your life com-plete to Him, And His

joy He'll place with-in, For the joy of the Lord is your strength.

Don't lose the joy of the Lord in your soul, For the

joy of the Lord is your strength. Let His Joy fill your soul,

And His Spir-it have con-trol, For the joy of the Lord is your strength.

183　Blessed Be the Name

Wm. H. Clark

Hudson

Bless-ed be the name, Bless-ed be the name, Bless-ed be the name of the Lord.

Bless-ed be the name, Bless-ed be the name, Bless-ed be the name of the Lord.

184　Lord, Make Me More Holy

Spiritual

Lord, make me more ho - ly, Lord, make me more ho - ly,

Lord, make me more ho - ly Un - til we meet a - gain.

Ho - ly, ho - ly, ho - ly, Un - til we meet a - gain.

2. Lord, make me more humble, 3. Lord, make me more loving,
4. Lord, keep us more faithful,

Singing on My Way to Heaven   185

I. S.

Iris Sutherland

With Joy

Sing-ing on my way to hea - ven; Sing-ing while I'm here be - low;

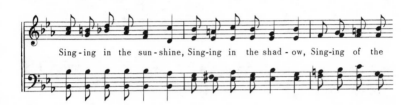

Sing-ing in the sun-shine, Sing-ing in the shad - ow, Sing-ing of the

Lord I know; When the days are filled with bless-ing,

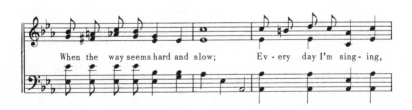

When the way seems hard and slow; Ev - ery day I'm sing - ing,

Prais-es ev - er bring - ing; Sing-ing for I love Him so!

186 God Said,"Set My People Free"

P. C. S. from Exodus 5:1

Phyllis C. Spiers

God said,"Set my peo-ple free, and let them go." God said,"Set my peo-ple free, and let them go." God said,"Set my peo-ple free, and let them go In - to the pro - mised land."

187 If You Really Love Him

If you real - ly love Him, You'll work and watch and pray; If you real - ly love Him, you'll serve Him ev - ery day; If you real - ly love Him, you'll nev - er go a - stray, If you real - ly love Him that way.

Everything's All Right in My Father's House

188

With joy

1. Ev - ery-thing's all right In my Fa -ther's house,
2. Come and go with me To my Fa - ther's house,
3. Je - sus is the way To my Fa - ther's house,

In my Fa - ther's house, In my Fa-ther's house. Ev - ery-thing's all
To my Fa- ther's house, To my Fa-ther's house. Come and go with
To my Fa- ther's house, To my Fa-ther's house. Je - sus is the

right In my Fa-ther's house.
me To my Fa-ther's house. There is joy, joy, joy.
way To my Fa-ther's house.

4. Singing will be there, 5. Clapping will be there, 6. Praising will be there,

Arr. Copyright © 1971 by Joy Music Co. in "Renewal in Song."

Praise Ye the Lord !

189

Psalm 117

With strength

Praise ye the Lord, Oh, praise the Lord all ye na - tions,

Praise Him all ye peo-ples; For His mer - ci - ful kind-ness is

great t'ward us, And the truth of the Lord en - dures for - ev - er!

Arr. Copyright © 1971 by Joy Music Co. in "Renewal in Song."

190   Everybody Ought to Know

Ev - ery-bod - y ought to know, (Ev - ery-bod - y ought to know) Ev - ery-
bod - y ought to know, (Ev - ery-bod - y ought to know) Ev - ery-
bod - y ought to know, (Ev - ery-bod - y ought to know) who Je - sus
is. (who Je - sus is) He's the Lil - y of the val -
ley, He's the bright and morn - ing Star,
He's the fair - est of ten thou - sand; Ev - ery-bod - y ought to know.

Right Now

Right now, right now, Let the Sav-iour bless your soul right now; Don't put off un-til to-mor-row what you can have to-day, Let the Sav-iour bless your soul right now.

The Grave Is Now Empty

A. A. A.

A. A. Anderson

The grave is now emp-ty, the stone rolled a-way, For Christ is a-live in my heart; And death which is con-quered in me has no part, For Christ is a-live in my heart.

193   Walking With the King

With joy

Hal - le - lu - jah, I'm walk-ing with the King, Praise His ho - ly name, Walk-ing with the King! Hal - le - lu - jah, I'm walk-ing with the King, Ev - ery day I'm walk-ing with the King!

194   If You'll Take My Jesus

W.H.W.

W. H. Wilson

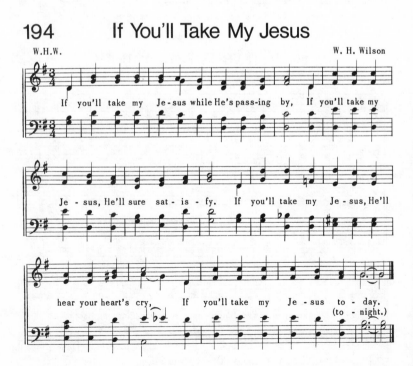

If you'll take my Je - sus while He's pass-ing by, If you'll take my Je - sus, He'll sure sat - is - fy. If you'll take my Je - sus, He'll hear your heart's cry, If you'll take my Je - sus to - day.
(to - night.)

With the High Praises of God   195

from Psalm 149:6

Vigorously

With the high prais-es of God in our mouth, And a two-edg- ed sword in our hand,

We will march right up on the vic-tors' side, Right in - to Ca-naan's land.

Free, Free, Free!   196

With strength

Free, free, free! Christ has set me free! Once I was

lost,   am found,
bound, but now I am free, I'm free,   free,   free!
blind   can see,

Why Not Now?   197

El Nathan   C. C. Case

Slowly

Why not now?   Why not now?   Why not come to Je-sus now?

Why not now?   Why not now?   Why not come to Je-sus now?

198 I'm Singing Wonderful! Wonderful!

I. S. With joy Iris Sutherland

I'm sing-ing Won-der-ful! Won-der-ful! Ev-ery day, in His way,

Won-der-ful! Won-der-ful is He; For Je-sus res-cued me,

set me free, Lift-ed me glo-rious-ly, Now I sing, Wonder-ful is He!

For I've come out of the val-ley where the dark-ness a-bounds;

I'm up on the moun-tain where the glo-ry is found; This my song

all day long, In the night or the fight, Won-der-ful! Won-der-ful is He!

The Joy of the Lord is My Strength   199

from Neh. 8:10, II Cor. 12:9

The joy of the Lord is my strength, The joy of the Lord is my strength. My strength is made per-fect, made per-fect in weak-ness. The joy of the Lord is my strength.

It's a Wonderful Day   200

B. R.

Bob Robin

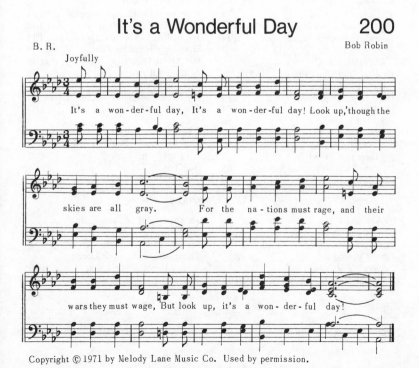

Joyfully

It's a won-der-ful day, It's a won-der-ful day! Look up, though the skies are all gray. For the na-tions must rage, and their wars they must wage, But look up, it's a won-der-ful day!

Topical Index

Titles Only
Our God

Our Worship

Our Response

TOPICAL INDEX, continued

General Index

Titles And First Words

GENERAL INDEX, continued